The Little Book
for a peaceful

To Dorothy and
Derek,

You are always
special cooperative
and giving souls.

Your benevolence is
a blessing to
everyone

ROGER COLE

Lothian
BOOKS

Thomas C. Lothian Pty Ltd
132 Albert Road, South Melbourne, Victoria 3205
www.lothian.com.au

Copyright © Roger Cole 2002
First published 2002

National Library of Australia
Cataloguing-in-Publication data:

Cole, Roger, 1955–.

Little book of blessings for a peaceful world.

ISBN 0 7344 0280 5.

1. Prayer-books. 2. Blessing and cursing. I. Title.

242

Design and typesetting by Kim Roberts Design
Colour reproduction by Scott Digital, Port Melbourne
Printed in Singapore by Craft Print International Ltd

Acknowledgements

I would like to acknowledge my mother, who had the courage to be different and uphold her spiritual values in this world. You are a blessing. There are few like you who give so much and ask for so little. I'll love you always.

Once again, I send my thanks to the Brahma Kumaris World Spiritual Organisation, to its leaders and members for their wisdom and knowledge, and the teachings of Raja Yoga meditation. I believe you have brought me closer to God. Royalties from the sale of this book are dedicated to the world-wide service of this organisation. If you wish to learn the meditation technique that inspired me to write these blessings, visit their web-page at www.brahmakumaris.com.au

To the patients and families I have cared for over the years, thank you for your struggles, your wisdom and your love. You have helped me to understand this world.

Introduction

We live in delicate times, in a world with too much sorrow and conflict. News of war, suffering, an untimely death or the victimisation of others affects us all deeply. Anger, sorrow or hatred seem to have replaced humankind's deepest wish for peace, love and happiness. We often feel helpless and inadequate, and unable to understand how human beings can behave like this. We feel impotent and unable to make a difference in a world that seems to have lost its moral values, its truth and its respect for human dignity. We fear that the world is moving towards its own destruction.

But there is something that each of us can do: we can stop limiting our minds and our consciousness. We can create a wish for world peace. Pure thoughts have power; as small packages they unravel their energy and reach the limits of the universe. If, together, we create pure thoughts of kindness and compassion, the light we bring to others will counter negative forces and bring peace and comfort to all the souls in this world.

To begin this transformation, educate, discipline and empower your own mind with positive thoughts about your eternal nature and identity. You are a great and beautiful being. Have you forgotten this truth? You have the power to create a peaceful world by becoming peaceful and co-operating with the divinity of pure values. Begin by accepting the blessings given here; take them deeply into your heart. They represent your true and forgotten *self*, which is a channel for unconditional love. Some may strengthen your mind to resist the negativity of people, news or circumstances. Others will give you new ways of interpreting and blessing the world around you. Overall, I hope they bring you happiness, and enable you to uphold the peaceful values that serve our world.

Let us each experience a personal power and potential we have lost sight of, and visualise a world returning to love. Set no limit on yourself; you are co-operating with God.

Angels

Be pure and light and show the path to God's love.

You are an angel, carefree and responsible.

You illuminate the path of truth.

As an angel, you are full of love and bless the world with truth.

Through the treasures of all virtues and the knowledge of your soul, you have the powerful realisation that you are becoming an angel.

Like an angel, you are an embodiment of truth, dispelling the darkness of ignorance.

With your angelic qualities, purity shines through your loving actions.

Your words are sweet and filled with the power of truth. You are an enlightened being with the heart of an angel.

Like an angel your vision reveals the love
of God.

With the eyes of an angel you spread the light of self-understanding in all directions. Your pure thoughts and good wishes empower all souls.

Like an angel your spirit shines with purity,
revealing the path to truth and self-realisation.

Benevolence

Forgive easily, have respect and give only love.

With pure feelings of benevolence and good wishes for everyone you attract souls to the divine.

You are a special soul who recognises truth.
Your awareness gives strength and hope to the
world.

You are an enlightened being who extends
unlimited love to the world.

Through spiritual knowledge your heart is constantly giving and reveals all virtues.

As an enlightened being you know that God sees only your perfection. Now see others as God sees you.

You are a generous soul filled with the power of love, whose giving is effortless and fulfilling.

By seeing only the highest qualities in everyone, you are a special soul who blesses the world with love.

As a wise and charitable soul, you uplift others through your words, your deeds and the power of pure thoughts.

Your pure thoughts and good wishes mirror
our divine potential and reflect our true nature.

Compassion

Always give love and be kind and understanding.

You are one whose compassion empowers
through your love and acceptance of others.

You feel compassion for all souls and realise the importance of time. It is time to embody truth and to give spiritual awareness to others.

You have the compassion to accept others and the understanding that they have been influenced by loss or fear.

You are the embodiment of compassion. Your healing presence dispels doubt and reveals the nature of your soul.

Never deceived by ego, your spirit is pure and
the embodiment of compassion.

The truth in your heart frees you from sorrow
and gives you compassion for all beings.

Your compassion liberates you from judgement and enables you to have divine insight and a loving vision of the world.

You are an enlightened being who has the compassion of an angel. With the light of truth you bring wisdom to all souls.

With unconditional love your compassion is
unlimited and heals all suffering.

Co-operation

Always be kind and work in harmony with others.

As an enlightened being who co-operates with all souls, you spread the beauty of your heart in all directions.

As a special angel you co-operate with divine love and remove sorrow from the world.

You are like an angel co-operating with God's love to bring peace to the world.

With the power of your mind you co-operate only with higher values that bring peace and happiness to your world.

Co-operating only with God's love, you never separate yourself from the task of creating a loving world.

Courage

Be true to yourself and uphold your highest values.

By understanding that your true nature is peace, you have the courage to uphold your highest values in a world of conflict.

Your courage has taken you beyond fear into the realisation of your soul. You now know yourself as God knows you.

Your courage and determination have freed you from worldly concerns. You are now a pure and creative being.

You are a great soul who has the courage to live by integrity and truth.

Your courage overcomes the attitudes that
challenge your faith and love for God.

Having found the courage to face and transform your weaknesses, you look on the world with strength and optimism.

Detachment

Remain peaceful, never affected yet always loving.

You are a soul who is both detached and loving.
Detached from negativity, you never withhold
your love.

Through deep faith you are peaceful and detached. Being in your presence is like standing before an angel.

By withdrawing from negativity, you maintain power in your awareness and constantly donate peace and happiness to the world.

Through detachment you have concentrated the power of peace in your soul. You are now gentle and easy in your relationships.

Detached from sorrow, you bring hope and comfort to the hearts of those who are suffering.

Your love and peace free you from sorrow and your faith keeps you detached and giving. You are now an instrument of divine love.

Faith

Know your spiritual identity and experience constant happiness.

With faith and understanding, you are a powerful soul whose thoughts radiate peace.

By accepting the divine order of life you are the embodiment of faith. You trust in God and have compassion for all beings.

With deep faith in the divine order of life, you have unshakeable peace and never use force.

Your gentleness and power reflect faith that is always trusting and never forceful.

The power to control your thoughts comes from the knowledge that you are a soul and the faith that there is divine order in the world.

With the faith of your eternal value, you are a powerful soul who is never influenced by self-doubt.

Forgiveness

Look on the world as innocent and blameless and in need of love.

With a forgiving heart you transform conflict
and arrogance into good wishes and
co-operation.

Through forgiveness you are free from grievances and bless the world with love.

With pure thoughts you are able to forgive and forget, and fly towards the loving light of God.

Your forgiveness shows others how to let go of the past and live happily in the moment.

With your forgiveness you recognise the innocence of all souls and give only love.

By seeing a blameless world you are a soul whose forgiveness reflects divine insight and closeness to God.

Honesty

Be true to yourself and always give love.

You are a soul with an honest heart and the integrity to be the same inside and out.

With a true and honest heart you are free to experience God's love and power.

You have a true heart and never feel separate from the divine.

With love for everyone, your honest and open
heart gives peace and hope to the world.

Your honest actions and words defuse conflict
and reveal pure spiritual values to the world.

You are a wise soul with a powerful intellect and an honest heart. You reveal truth to the world and remain humble.

Humility

Live by your own truth and accept everyone as they are.

You are an angel who flies on the wings of humility and self-respect. You shine with light and truth.

Your humility attunes you to God's love and power and makes you an instrument who reveals divine understanding to the world.

With your sweetness, love and humility, there is compassion and truth in your words.

Knowing yourself to be an instrument, you remain humble and constantly serve the needs of others.

Through humility you have become a divine
instrument and an example for the world.

With your humility and mercy you have become an instrument of love and a messenger of peace.

Innocence

Be happy for no reason and give happiness to everyone.

As a trustee you have no worries of ownership
and simply take care of everything for God.

With childlike innocence and a desire to benefit others you embody simplicity and truth.

Through reawakening your innocence you are completely uncomplicated and loved by everyone.

Your innocent nature makes you trustworthy
because you are unconditional with your love.

Letting go

Be free of all limitations.

By letting go, you have become peaceful and free to fly into the loving heart of God.

By letting go of your desire for recognition, you live in your own beauty and serve the world with love.

Free from doubt and selfish desires, you have
let go of the past and accept yourself as a
worthy child of God.

By letting go of all expectations, you bless the world with unconditional love, trust and acceptance.

By letting go of ego, you are free and your inner happiness uplifts the world around you.

Not needing to impress anyone, you remain
calm and creative and bless the world with love.

Love

To become the love that you are, always give
the love that you want.

Radiating pure love, you are an instrument of peace and unity.

Free from fear and sorrow, your heart reveals
only love to the world.

You are a special being who has drawn the power of divine love into your soul.

You have surrendered your ego and become an instrument of God's love.

You are joined to everyone with a thread of love and like an ocean of love you are at one with all beings.

By becoming love itself you create unity and
heal the illusion of separateness.

By letting go of fear and becoming an image of love, your presence is one of forgiveness and acceptance.

Through belonging to God you are a special angel. Your love reveals truth and brings about self-realisation.

Love is your form, love is your awareness and love is your being. In the image of love you have the power to reflect the divine nature of all beings.

Peace

Be gentle and understanding and bring peace to the world.

By recognising the peace of your soul, you have become an instrument for peace in the world.

You are a peaceful soul who uplifts and lightens the spirits of others.

Revealing pure thoughts and pure feelings in your eyes, you are a messenger of peace and truth to the world.

You are an angel who flies on the wings of
God's love and spreads peace to the world.

Through your acceptance of others, you have an easy nature and the power to remain peaceful.

Liberated from negative influences and wasteful thoughts, you are a peace messenger in this world.

Power

Be the master of your thoughts and create a beautiful life.

Your power to control your thoughts ends
negativity and creates an atmosphere of love
and stability.

By remembering God, you receive the power of your angelic form and become an instrument of love in this world.

Through the truth of your soul, you experience the power of divine love and are never affected by the anger of others.

You are your own master, with the power to control your mind and your physical senses.

You are a soul who has full control over your mind and the thoughts you create. No one can make you unhappy.

Your power to control your thoughts keeps you free from negative influences. Your spiritual feelings can now emerge and transform the world with love.

Purity

Sparkle like a diamond and make this a beautiful world.

With a true heart and pure thoughts you reveal
the way to God.

Filled with the power of divine love, you are a soul whose pure thoughts bring peace to the world.

Filled with the pure desire for eternal peace and happiness, your powerful thoughts send a message of peace to all souls.

As a pure being, you uphold your virtues, fill your heart with peace and give only love to the world.

With the power of pure thoughts your mind is an instrument to heal and serve others.

You are a peaceful soul and a child of God.
You have rediscovered the purity of your
eternal nature.

Your gentle eyes are powerful and revealing.

As windows to your soul, they show the world

your purity and peace.

Respect

Look only for goodness in others and uphold the value of human life.

Like the reed, you have the strength and flexibility to accommodate all storms. You bend but never break, then stand tall in your self-respect.

Through your respect for all beings, you are a
soul who inspires others to seek their highest
truth.

Through your self-respect you constantly donate positive, pure thoughts and feelings to the world.

With your humility and self-respect you make others feel valued.

By seeing divine potential in everyone, you inspire their transformation and bring them happiness.

Through self-respect you rise above fear and
negativity, with a loving presence that heals the
world.

Serenity

Be in harmony with yourself and accommodate everyone with love.

You have the stainless inner beauty of serenity, and your presence is filled with compassion and truth.

Your deep serenity and wisdom bring strength and hope to all you meet.

With purity and peace you are a serene and powerful influence on the world.

Like a spiritual flower you are serene and fragrant with all virtues. You colour the world with your spirituality.

Your deep serenity comes from peace and from knowing your eternal relationship with God.

By allowing love to transform your life you are
serene, with the nature of an angel.

Surrender

Be surrendered and take refuge in God's love.

Your eyes reveal the simplicity and power of your total surrender to God. Your loving form heals the world.

By surrendering to love, you have let go of fear and self-doubt and become an instrument of the divine.

Through surrender you are free from attachment and dependency. You can now be happy and light.

By letting go and surrendering to God's love
you now belong to God, and the power of His
love goes with you.

Like a moth you have surrendered yourself in the flame of God's love. God's power is with you always.

Tolerance

Be good-natured and accept everyone with love.

Your power to tolerate comes from your understanding that all souls have forgotten God's love.

With faith in God and the divine order of all things, you are a powerful soul who cannot be influenced by the words and actions of others.

You are one who tolerates without strain or tension. Your power of tolerance comes from a loving heart that accommodates everyone.

You understand that sorrow and deprivation are the roots of wrong action. With this acceptance you heal and transform others.

With tolerance born of acceptance and understanding, you look at the world with merciful vision.

Transformation

Change yourself and inspire the world to change with you.

Illuminating the path of self-realisation, you are an angel who brings transformation and truth to the world.

With your pure thoughts and acceptance of others you uplift souls and help them to move forward. By never seeing their weaknesses you inspire their transformation.

Your power of self-realisation reveals the truth of your eternal being and brings about transformation in others.

With divine vision and acceptance you see others without judgement and create gentle transformation of the world you live in.

Through awareness of love you are undergoing complete self-transformation. As an instrument of the divine, you bring loving transformation to the world.

Truth

With unconditional love you awaken others to their highest potential.

As a lamp in the darkness, your soul gives safe passage and reveals the destiny of truth.

Through truth you are a divine being whose pure actions reveal only love.

Your truth and wisdom radiate from a pure heart and divine intellect.

Truth gives you an angelic presence revealing your pure and divine qualities.

Truth and acceptance emanate from your pure
and loving heart.

Wisdom

Reawaken your innocence by discovering your virtues.

By knowing yourself as a soul, you are gentle, honest and wise.

Having recognised that all difficulties come
to teach you, you are wise, and free to fly like
an angel.

Never deceived by doubt or desire, you are a wise soul whose vision is always on the eternal.

Divine knowledge and experience have given you a clear and wise intellect.

World peace

First find peace within yourself, then bring peace to our world.

As a being of love, you are a divine instrument who reveals love to all souls. Your loving nature heals and blesses the world with peace.

As an instrument for world peace, you have to change yourself, then let God do the rest.

By creating peace within yourself, you have the power to create peace in the world.

You are one who understands that chaos in the world precedes divine order and lasting peace. You remain unshakeable and stable in the company of God's love.

Om Shanti